Fact Finders®

PERSPECTIVES on HISTORY

MARIE ANTOINETTE

FASHIONABLE QUEEN OR GREEDY ROYAL?

by Sarah Webb

Consultant:
Frank Anselmo, PhD
Department of French Studies
Louisiana State University

CAPSTONE PRESS
a capstone imprint

Fact Finders Books are published by Capstone Press,
1710 Roe Crest Drive, North Mankato, Minnesota 56003
www.capstonepub.com

Library of Congress Cataloging-in-Publication Data
Webb, Sarah Powers, 1967–
Marie Antoinette: fashionable queen or greedy royal? / by Sarah Powers Webb.
pages cm. — (Fact finders. Perspectives on history)
Summary: "Details the life of Marie Antoinette from differing perspectives"— Provided by
publisher.
Includes bibliographical references and index.
ISBN 978-1-4914-2041-6 (library binding)
ISBN 978-1-4914-2216-8 (paperback)
ISBN 978-1-4914-2231-1 (eBook PDF)
1. Marie Antoinette, Queen, consort of Louis XVI, King of France, 1755–1793—Juvenile literature.
2. Queens—France—Biography—Juvenile literature. 3. France—History—Louis XVI, 1774–1793—
Juvenile literature. I. Title.
DC137.1.W365 2015
944'.035092—dc23
[B]   2014028914

Editorial Credits
Brenda Haugen, editor; Heidi Thompson, designer; Svetlana Zhurkin, media researcher; Laura
Manthe, production specialist

Photo Credits
Alamy: Mary Evans Picture Library, 14; CRIAimages: Jay Robert Nash Collection, cover (middle
right), 21; iStockphotos: GeorgiosArt, 23; Newscom: akg-images, 7 (top), 11, 17, 18, 25, 29, Album/
Oronoz, 8, Album/Prisma, 27, SIPA/E.R.L., 5; Shutterstock: abadesign, cover (background),
Daniela Migliorisi, 13; SuperStock: Fine Art Images, cover (bottom)

Design Elements by Shutterstock

Direct Quotes
p. 9 from *Marie Antoinette: The Journey* by Antonia Fraser (New York: N.A. Talese/Doubleday, 2001)
p. 17 from *Marie Antoinette: The Last Queen of France* by Evelyne Lever (New York: Farrar, Straus,
and Giroux, 2000)
p. 26 from *Marie Antoinette: The Journey*

Printed in China by Nordica.
1014/CA21401513
092014   008470NORDS15

TABLE OF CONTENTS

A Date with the Executioner

Marie Antoinette, the former queen of France, waited in the damp, dark cell of the prison as the sun rose October 16, 1793. She had not slept at all the night before. Her lady-in-waiting softly greeted her. She helped Marie change into a clean dress. Months in prison had left Marie pale and thin.

The executioner tied the queen's hands behind her back. As the prison guards took her outside, she almost fainted. There was no carriage to meet her. Instead she rode in a common cart like a criminal, facing backward.

The cart traveled through the crowded streets for more than an hour. Some people insulted and shouted at the queen as she rode by. She did not react.

Finally the cart halted in front of a platform. Above Marie a shiny blade hung between two heavy beams. It was a **guillotine**. In a few moments, the queen would lose her head.

Who was Marie Antoinette? Some said she was a criminal who deserved to die. Others claimed she was just a victim of politics. What events led the queen to her death?

guillotine: machine for executing people by beheading them

Marie Antoinette faced her death with dignity.

FORMING AN ALLIANCE

Maria Antonia Josephina Johanna was born November 2, 1755, in Vienna, Austria. Her mother, Empress Maria Theresa, ruled the Habsburg Empire. She called her daughter Antonia. The girl grew up in the royal Hofburg Palace. She led a childhood of pleasure and wealth. Her tutors tried to help her study, but they often cut her lessons short. Antonia mostly liked to play.

Empress Maria had big plans for her daughter. She wanted an **alliance** with France. Austria and France had long been enemies. The empress hoped a royal marriage would keep peace between the two countries. By the time Antonia was 13, her mother had arranged for her to marry the **dauphin** of France, Louis Auguste. He was the grandson of France's king. Antonia had to follow her mother's wishes. She was powerless to decide her own future.

alliance: an agreement between nations or groups of people to work together

dauphin: the male next in line to be the king of France; the dauphine is the wife of the dauphin

Antonia (third from left) grew up in a wealthy family.

London ★

Netherlands

Belgium

Paris ★

Versailles

France

Switzerland

Vienna ★

Habsburg Empire

Italy

Spain

Antonia married Louis surrounded by the French king and his royal family.

Antonia married Louis Auguste on May 16, 1770, in the Royal Chapel at Versailles, France. She was just 14 years old. He was only 15. They had met just before the wedding. The French called the young bride Marie Antoinette, or Madame La Dauphine. She never saw her mother or her homeland again.

FACT

When she got married, Antonia had to leave her dog, Mops, behind in Austria. She later had him join her in France.

A DAUGHTER'S PLACE

Antonia was the 15th of 16 children. Empress Maria Theresa believed her young daughters should do whatever she told them to do. She said, "They are born to obey and must learn to do so in good time."

Many of Empress Theresa's sons and daughters married princes and princesses from other countries. Among them were Spain and Bavaria. It was typical at that time for noble children to have marriages arranged by their parents. The marriages formed alliances. Kingdoms needed alliances to protect their borders from enemies.

As a new dauphine, Marie Antoinette had one job. She had to give birth to a male child. An **heir** would continue the royal family. But the couple did not start a family right away.

Louis Auguste and Marie Antoinette spent a lot of time apart. They were both so young and very different. Louis was terribly shy and timid. Marie was charming and bubbly. She liked to attend late night masked balls, parties, and theater. Louis enjoyed hunting during the day and went to bed early. He loved reading about history, geography, and science. His wife preferred to play rather than study. Where she was graceful, he was clumsy. He was tall but chubby and waddled when he walked. Marie walked like she was floating on air.

AN EXPENSIVE WARDROBE

The clothing of an entire French working class family cost about 30 livres. Wealthy nobles spent an average of 2,000 to 5,000 livres on their clothes. By comparison, Empress Theresa spent 400,000 livres on Marie Antoinette's clothing to prepare for her wedding. The empress knew her daughter needed dresses made of the finest fabrics. Marie wore a silver brocade wedding gown covered with white diamonds. A livre in Marie Antoinette's day was worth between $20 to $30 today. That means Marie Antoinette traveled to France with clothes valued around $8 million to $12 million.

Marie played the spinet,
a piano-like instrument.

heir: someone who has been or will be left a title, property, or money

Chapter 2

BECOMING THE QUEEN

The dauphin of France, Louis Auguste, became King Louis XVI on May 10, 1774. Just 19 years old, Marie Antoinette was now the queen of France. In public the French people appeared to like the new queen and king. But in private people were suspicious of the new queen. They called her "the Austrian woman." French nobles believed that Marie Antoinette would try to control the French king with her Austrian advice.

In truth Marie had no desire to control the king's politics, but she did enjoy his wealth. As queen Marie believed she could behave any way she wanted. She spent many evenings playing cards and gambling. She often giggled at important events.

FACT

Marie Antoinette hated the public life at Versailles. Any commoner could be admitted to the court—and the royal rooms—as long as they were dressed well. People could watch her dress, undress, and eat. Up to 10,000 people a day visited Versailles.

Marie also spent money **lavishly**. She held two costume balls a week at the royal palace in Versailles. At times there may have been between 2,000 and 4,000 other nobles living with the royal family at the palace. The palace was also called Versailles. The costume balls were expensive events. It did not help Marie's public image that the king gave her a private palace. It was called Le Petit Trianon.

Le Petit Trianon included several buildings and gardens.

lavish: spending or giving more than is necessary

Marie sometimes dressed as a shepherdess at Trianon.

PLAYING AT HER PALACE

At Le Petit Trianon, Marie Antoinette had a fake country village built. It included peasant houses, a farmhouse, and a dairy. She used her village for outdoor theater games. She often played the role of a peasant.

Marie's behavior at Trianon offended older nobles. They viewed her play as childish. They thought she showed disrespect for the throne. Both nobles and commoners did not like that she could hide in her private palace. The queen spent days at Trianon and returned to Versailles at night.

Many people misunderstood Marie. At Versailles she had to follow more rules. They required her to eat with certain people and dress a particular way. At Trianon Marie had more control. She invited only the people she wished to see. Marie hated the stuffy, strict Versailles palace. She wanted a simpler life away from all the rules of Versailles.

Marie also loved helping children and the poor. A poor boy named Jacques once fell under Marie's carriage. Marie jumped out of the coach to help him. Learning the boy was an orphan, Marie adopted him. Servants raised him at Versailles. In other instances Marie asked her husband to be generous with his money and give it to good causes.

These kind actions went unnoticed. In four years as queen, Marie had made many enemies. Nobles felt the queen did not respect the French people and ignored too many rules.

FACT

Mean stories and rumors about Marie were sometimes printed in booklets called *libelles*. Stories in the booklets **exaggerated** her actions. Many people learned about Marie only from these booklets.

exaggerate: to make something bigger or more important than it really is

Chapter 3

A LAVISH LIFESTYLE

After seven years the royal couple still had no children. Gossip about being childless threatened Marie's authority. During this time the queen used fashion to establish her power. She ordered the finest silk dresses and outfits. She bought 200 to 300 new outfits per year. She purchased four new pairs of shoes each week. Her clothes took up three rooms at Versailles.

Marie also developed a unique hairstyle called a pouf. This hairstyle included ribbons, flowers, ostrich feathers, or scenes. The fancy poufs sometimes reached 3 feet (0.9 meters) in height. One themed hairstyle included artichokes, carrots, radishes, and even a head of cabbage. Her pouf became a symbol of reckless spending.

French nobles said hateful things about Marie behind her back. Commoners accused her of spending too much money. People did not think Marie acted like a queen. They thought she was silly and wasteful.

Marie dressed in elaborate gowns and had her hair done in a pouf.

A Musical Insult

Nobles sang a song about Marie Antoinette to show how they felt about her.

"Little 20-year-old queen/Since you treat people with no shame/You'll go back from where you came."

Marie wore fancy gowns though many people in France were starving.

Marie Antoinette misjudged people. She did not understand how the poor felt about her spending. People wrote about her expensive clothes and parties. Marie often changed dresses three times each day. She usually wore her fancy gowns just once.

Like other nobles, Marie spent a lot of money. But rules required nobles to live lavishly. She also had no control over the king's politics. By the late 1770s France had already spent a lot of money fighting wars against England in America. But the *libelles* blamed France's money problems on Marie's expensive lifestyle.

A TASTE FOR EQUALITY

During the last half of the 1700s, people read about the Enlightenment philosophy in France. Authors wrote that all people were equal. In 1776 the United States adopted the Declaration of Independence and went to war against the British king. France helped the United States, which won its independence in 1783. French soldiers brought back news about the new American government. Feelings against the French **monarchy** were growing among commoners.

monarchy: a type of government in which a king or queen is head of state

Chapter 4

MADAME DEFICIT

Between 1774 and 1787 people in France experienced severe hunger. Poor harvests and harsh winters caused wheat shortages, which meant no flour for bread. Food riots broke out. Workers grew restless against the monarchy. People blamed Marie for many of their problems. They called her "Madame **Deficit**." They said she spent money recklessly. But the money she spent was just a small part of the problem. The king spent too much money helping the Americans win their independence. Many people did not know this. The king controlled what the newspapers printed about him and his policies.

FACT

During the unrest, Marie supposedly asked why the people rioted. An aide said it was because of bread shortages, since flour was scarce. Some claimed that Marie replied, "Let them eat cake." However, there is no evidence that she actually made this statement. It did not help Marie's image that a main ingredient in hair powder for her poufs was flour.

deficit: the loss created when government spends more than it takes in

Meanwhile Marie Antoinette finally had a son, an heir to the throne. Between 1778 and 1786, Marie gave birth to four children— Marie Therese Charlotte, Louis Joseph, Louis Charles, and Sophie Helene Beatrice. *Libelles* still wrote hateful things about Marie. They suggested the king was not the father of her children.

a painting of Marie and three of her children

A 1785 scandal also damaged Marie's reputation. A jealous court noble, Comtesse Lamotte, tricked a **cardinal** into a theft scheme. Lamotte told the cardinal that the queen wanted an expensive diamond necklace. The cardinal told a jeweler the queen would pay for the necklace. The cardinal picked up the necklace, but Lamotte's husband fled the country with it. Police put Comtesse Lamotte in jail. A trial found the cardinal not guilty of any wrongdoing. However, this event forever hurt Marie Antoinette's image. She never wanted the necklace. Even so, French citizens believed the queen was behind the whole scheme. They believed she was uncaring and would rather spend money on diamonds than help the starving people.

In 1787, after what came to be known as the Diamond Necklace Affair, Marie finally began to reduce her spending. She was tired of all the hurtful writing. Some French people said that the queen's love of fashion was proof of her cruel nature. Marie stopped wearing so many fancy poufs and silk dresses. She ordered plain dresses made out of cotton. Yet nobles still criticized her choices. They thought cotton dresses made her look like a peasant.

cardinal: an official of the Roman Catholic Church next in rank to the pope

Marie couldn't escape criticism even when she wore less expensive clothes.

23

Her fashion changes also hurt French workers. After Marie quit ordering fancy dresses, several silk factories were unable to pay their debts. Many people lost their jobs. She also bought cotton fabric from England. As a result, people accused Marie of not supporting the French economy. Workers thought she was blind to their troubles of joblessness and hunger.

The people of France could no longer contain their anger. A mob stormed the Bastille, a prison in Paris, on July 14, 1789. The angry men hoped gunpowder could be found there. The tide had turned. A **revolution** against the monarchy had begun.

Women later became involved in the uprising too. Their families were starving. They thought the king and queen selfishly hid flour and bread at Versailles. On October 5, 1789, a mob of women walked 12 miles (19.3 kilometers) from Paris to Versailles. They demanded lower food prices from the king. Women stormed the palace and destroyed the queen's rooms. By October 6, the women marched back to Paris with the royal family as prisoners. They also carried huge supplies of grain with them. The people thought they could get the king to listen to their complaints. They viewed Marie as a monster. They blamed her for their suffering.

revolution: violent uprising by the people of a country that changes its system of government

republic: a form of government in which the people have the power to elect representatives who manage the government

Parisian marketwomen marched to Versailles and took the royal family as prisoners.

The royal family lived under heavy guard in the Tuileries Palace in Paris from 1789 to 1791. They still lived comfortably, but they did not have the same freedom they had before. The king was still technically in charge of the country, but he lost more and more power over time.

It was a dangerous time. The queen did not believe her husband should give in to the people's demands for equality. She thought that divine rule should be saved at all costs. Both the king and queen pretended to support the causes of the revolution. But they secretly wrote letters to other countries asking for support. Marie hoped her Austrian homeland would send an army to defeat the revolution.

It had also been a heart-breaking time. The royals had lost their son Louis Joseph on June 4, 1789. He likely died of some form of tuberculosis, a disease that often attacks the lungs but may have attacked his spine. Marie later said of that summer, "At the death of my poor little dauphin, the nation hardly seemed to notice."

Commoners, people who weren't part of the royal family, took control of the government in late 1789. The next year the new government put an end to all noble titles. The king became Louis Capet, from his family name.

Guards moved the royal family to the Temple, a Paris prison, in 1792. The new French government tried Louis Capet and found him guilty of **treason**. He was **executed** by guillotine January 21, 1793.

The king said good-bye to his family before he was executed.

treason: the crime of betraying one's government

execute: to put to death

Chapter 5

THE WIDOW CAPET

About nine months after her husband was executed, Marie was living in La Conciergerie, another prison in Paris. Now called the Widow Capet, Marie faced charges including treason. On October 15, 1793, a court found her guilty and sentenced her to death. The sentence would be carried out that very day.

The prison cart rolled to a stop near the guillotine. To the cheers of the Paris crowd, the blade fell quickly. Marie's life had ended. She was 37 years old.

What was the truth of Marie Antoinette's life? Her only job was to have a son. Did she have the authority to help the commoners? Did she make things worse with her lavish lifestyle?

Marie's mother forced her into an arranged marriage. New beliefs about French government arose during this time. People wanted to get rid of the monarchy. The new government accused her of treason. Was she really a criminal who deserved to die? Did the revolution encourage the court to execute her? Or was she just a victim of politics?

Marie listened as her death sentence was read.

GLOSSARY

alliance (uh-LY-uhnts)—an agreement between nations or groups of people to work together

cardinal (KAR-duh-nuhl)—an official of the Roman Catholic Church next in rank to the pope

dauphin (DO-fan)—the male next in line to be the king of France; the dauphine (DO-feen) is the wife of the dauphin

deficit (DEF-uh-sit)—the loss created when government spends more than it takes in

exaggerate (ig-ZAJ-uh-rayt)—to make something bigger or more important than it really is

execute (EK-suh-KYOOT)—to put to death

guillotine (GIL-uh-teen)—machine for executing people by beheading them

heir (AIR)—someone who has been or will be left a title, property, or money

lavish (LAV-ish)—spending or giving more than is necessary

monarchy (MON-ahr-kee)—a type of government in which a king or queen is head of state

republic (ri-PUHB-lik)—a form of government in which the people have the power to elect representatives who manage the government

revolution (rev-uh-LOO-shun)—violent uprising by the people of a country that changes its system of government

treason (TREE-zuhn)—the crime of betraying one's government

READ MORE

Colson, Mary. *France*. Countries Around the World. Chicago: Heinemann Library, 2012.

Hockinson, Liz. *Marie Antoinette: "Madame Deficit."* Thinking Girl's Treasury of Dastardly Dames. Foster City, Ca.: Goosebottom Books, 2011.

Lasky, Kathryn. *Marie Antoinette: Princess of Versailles*. New York: Scholastic, 2000.

INTERNET SITES

FactHound offers a safe, fun way to find Internet sites related to this book. All of the sites on FactHound have been researched by our staff.

Here's all you do:

Visit *www.facthound.com*

Type in this code: 9781491420416

 Check out projects, games and lots more at
www.capstonekids.com

CRITICAL THINKING USING THE COMMON CORE

1. Booklets from the 1780s called Marie Antoinette the "Queen of Vice." Explain what you think they meant by that. Use details from the text to support your response. (Key Ideas and Details)

2. How do the chapter titles illustrate Marie Antoinette's life? Use details from the text to support your answer. (Craft and Structure)

3. The Enlightenment philosophy encouraged freedom from a monarchy. The people fought for a republic. A republic is a government where the people have the power to elect representatives to make laws. Do you think Marie Antoinette had to die to create a French republic? (Integration of Knowledge and Ideas)

INDEX